Wallaby and Wallaroo Care

A Complete Owner's Guide

Raising, Breeding, Facts, Habitat, Diet, Care, Health, and Where to Buy
All included

By Lolly Brown

Foreword

The kangaroo stands out in popular perception as the world's most famous marsupial. There are, in fact, 334 species of marsupials found around the world, including the opossum in North America.

While arguably not as cute as a joey peeking out of its mother's pouch, the sight of 8 or 9 baby "possums" clinging to their mother as she waddles along can't help but make you crack a smile.

This whimsicality is something all marsupials seem to share. Whether it's their oddly matter-of-fact expressions, their half-hopping walk, or their full-out bounding leaps that first attract your attention, roos are irresistible.

In the world of exotic pets, however, having a kangaroo is a difficult proposition unless you have a great deal of land and good fencing. Some species of kangaroo can reach 7 feet (2.13 meters) in height!

Wallabies and wallaroos, on the other hand, are more reasonably sized for companion animals. Wallabies, which are sometimes thought of as "mini kangaroos" stand around 3.5 feet / 1 meter and less, while wallaroos are slightly larger at 5 feet / 1.5 meters and less.

All marsupials are unique in the animal kingdom because their young do not develop for an extended period of time in a placenta. Instead, at birth, the tiny baby, called a "joey," climbs up into its mother's pouch where it attaches to a nipple and continues its growth.

When you adopt either a wallaby or a wallaroo, you will be bringing home a joey. The level of care required for these little animals is similar to that needed by a newborn human infant.

Also, factor in the necessity to travel to the breeder's facility to retrieve your new pet for adoption. Don't expect anyone to ship a joey to you. They're too sensitive and delicate to survive the process. In fact, if you find a breeder that offers to ship, rethink the arrangement.

During the first year of your pet's life, it can probably live inside, but after that, a sizable outdoor enclosure will be needed. While wallabies and wallaroos can come inside, and enjoy doing so, they aren't house pets and they can't be housebroken.

Before you consider giving in to the lure of either animal, be sure that you understand its requirements in terms of housing and diet -- and ensure that you can meet those requirements.

To some extent, keeping either a wallaby or a wallaroo is more akin to having "livestock" than a "pet" in the conventional sense of the word.

They are grazing animals, and they need room to run and play. If you are in rural circumstances, and local laws do not forbid it, you're in a good position to consider these animals as pets.

When bottle-raised, both wallabies and wallaroos are gentle, affectionate, and loyal pets and are relatively long-lived, usually surviving 10-15 years.

In the following text, I try to provide all the necessary information to help you decide if either a wallaby or a wallaroo is a good fit for your life.

I'd like to tell you that it's the absolute definitive word on wallaby and wallaroo care, but the truth is that the longer you live with these animals the more they will teach you. Even people who have been working with wallabies and wallaroos for years admit they are still learning new lessons.

This is, for many, part of the great appeal of keeping these animals as pets. If, at the end of this reading, you decide that you want to join the ranks of those people, be prepared for an adventure!

Wallabies and wallaroos have a particular talent for working their way into your heart and staying there for life.

Acknowledgments

I would like to express my gratitude towards my family, friends, and colleagues for their kind co-operation and encouragement which helped me in completion of this book.

I would like to express my special gratitude and thanks to my loving husband for his patience, understanding, and support.

My thanks and appreciations also go to my colleagues and people who have willingly helped me out with their abilities.

Additional thanks to my children, whose love and care for our family pets inspired me to write this book.

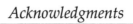

Acknowledgments

Table of Contents

Table of Contents

Ch. 1) - Understanding Wallabies and Wallaroos

Wallabies and wallaroos are marsupials in the family *Macropodidae*. This group of "macropods," a name literally meaning "large foot," also includes kangaroos, tree-kangaroos and pademelons.

Macropods as a group are native to Australia, New Guinea, and the neighboring islands. Prior to the European settlement of Australia, there were more than 50 different species of macropods.

Six species have now become extinct, and an additional 11 have greatly dropped in population density due to habitat loss, climate change, and predation among other factors.

1) Wallaby vs. Wallaroo

The term "wallaby" does not refer to a particular species. Rather, it is a categorization used to define a number of macropods of moderate size. There are about thirty different species that fall into the "wallaby" category and they are differentiated into groups including:

- **Typical Wallabies** – genus *Macropus*, most closely related to kangaroos and Wallaroos
- **Pademelons** – forest-dwelling wallabies, genus *Thylogale*
- **Rock-Wallabies** – genus *Petrogale*
- **Banded Hare-Wallaby** – *Lagostrophus fasciatus*

The most general difference between wallaroos and wallabies is their size. Wallabies are typically small to medium-sized with thick-set bodies. Wallaroos are only slightly smaller than kangaroos, but also have thick-set bodies.

Both animals exhibit a similar upright stance with tucked elbows and bent wrists as well as large hind feet.

More significant differences can be seen between wallaroos and the various types of wallaby. Rock-wallabies, for example, tend to live on rugged terrain, using their rough feet to grip the rock.

Pademelons are typically found in forested regions and are some of the smallest marsupials on Earth. They have similar body structure to the wallaroo, but with shorter, thicker tails that are sparsely haired.

Consequently, the list of "types" of wallabies is quite long:

Agile wallaby, *Macropus agilis*
Allied rock-wallaby, *Petrogale assimilis*
Banded hare-wallaby, *Lagostrophus fasciatus*
Black dorcopsis, *Dorcopsis atrata*
Black-flanked rock-wallaby, *Petrogale lateralis*
Black-striped wallaby, *Macropus dorsalis*
Bridled nail-tail wallaby, *Onychogalea fraenata*
Brown dorcopsis, *Dorcopsis muelleri*
Brown's pademelon, *Thylogale browni*
Brush-tailed rock-wallaby, *Petrogale penicillata*
Calaby's pademelon, *Thylogale calabyi*
Cape York rock-wallaby, *Petrogale coenensis*
Crescent nail-tail wallaby, *Onychogalea lunata* (extinct)

Dusky pademelon, *Thylogale brunii*
Eastern hare-wallaby, *Lagorchestes leporides* (extinct)
Godman's rock-wallaby, *Petrogale godmani*
Gray dorcopsis, *Dorcopsis luctuosa*
Herbert's rock-wallaby, *Petrogale herberti*
Macleay's dorcopsis, *Dorcopsulus macleayi*
Mareeba rock-wallaby, *Petrogale mareeba*
Monjon, *Petrogale burbidgei*
Mt. Claro rock-wallaby, *Petrogale sharmani*
Mountain pademelon, *Thylogale lanatus*
Nabarlek, *Petrogale concinna*
Northern nail-tail wallaby, *Onychogalea unguifera*
Parma wallaby, *Macropus parma* (rediscovered, thought extinct for 100 years)
Proserpine rock-wallaby, *Petrogale persephone*
Purple-necked rock-wallaby, *Petrogale purpureicollis*
Red-legged pademelon, *Thylogale stigmatica*
Red-necked pademelon, *Thylogale thetis*
Red-necked wallaby, *Macropus rufogriseus*
Rothschild's rock-wallaby, *Petrogale rothschildi*
Rufous hare-wallaby, *Lagorchestes hirsutus*
Short-eared rock-wallaby, *Petrogale brachyotis*
Swamp wallaby or Black Wallaby, *Wallabia bicolor*
Tammar wallaby, *Macropus eugenii*
Tasmanian pademelon, *Thylogale billardierii*
Toolache wallaby, *Macropus greyii* (extinct)
Unadorned rock-wallaby, *Petrogale inornata*
Western brush wallaby, *Macropus irma*
Whiptail wallaby, *Macropus parryi*
White-striped dorcopsis, *Dorcopsis hageni*
Yellow-footed rock-wallaby, *Petrogale xanthopus*

The Bennett's or Red Necked Wallaby, indigenous to Tasmania and mainland Australia, is the type most typically kept as a pet.

These animals grow to a size of 35-60 lbs. / 16-27 kg and stand 2-3 feet / 0.6-0.9 meters tall when fully grown. Their lifespan is 10-15 years, but some individuals in captivity have reached 19-20 years of age. They are reasonably hardy in colder climates and come in both grey and albino varieties.

This text will use the term "wallaby" in a somewhat generalized fashion with the assumption that you will be caring for an animal like the Bennett's Wallaby.

2) Understanding Wallaroos

The name "wallaroo" is actually a portmanteau of "kangaroo" and "wallaby," though native Australians generally do not use this name. The greatest distinguishing feature in all of these animals is size.

If you were to use the terms in ascending order from smallest to largest you would have:

- wallaby
- wallaroo
- kangaroo

In Australia, large, slim-bodied macropods are referred to as kangaroos while smaller, thick-set species are called wallabies. Therefore, in its native land, the wallaroo is just a little smaller than a kangaroo.

There are three major species of wallaroo, all typically found in open country, and a number of sub-species. All share similar characteristics with their kangaroo and wallaby relatives.

Wallaroos, like kangaroos and wallabies, are known for their upright stance with wrists raised and tucked elbows. They move by hopping with their large hind feet, balancing with their long tails.

Though wallaroos are wild animals, they are becoming more popular as pets, with more professional breeders offering animals for sale. In Australia, it is not uncommon for individuals to rescue orphaned wallaroo babies and to raise them by hand.

Wallaroos are not just cute and cuddly as pets, they are also very affectionate and entertaining to have around.

3) Types of Wallaroos

There are three major species of Wallaroo:

- Common Wallaroo (*Macropus robustus*)
- Black Wallaroo (*Macropus bernardus*)
- Antilopine Wallaroo (*Macropus antilopinus*)

The Common Wallaroo is also sometimes referred to as the Hill Kangaroo or the Hill Wallaroo. There are four subspecies of Common Wallaroo found in various parts of Australia excluding Tasmania.

a.) Common Wallaroo (*Macropus robustus*)

The four subspecies of *Macropus robustus* are categorized based on differences in color, size and genetics.

- *Macropus robustus robustus* (Eastern Wallaroo)
- *Macropus robustus erubescens* (Euro)
- *Macropus robustus woodwardi* (Northern Wallaroo)
- *Macropus robustus isabellinus* (Barrow Island Euro)

The Barrow Island Euro is the most distinctive of the four subspecies, having a smaller and stockier build. These wallaroos may reach only half the size of other species. The Eastern wallaroo and the Euro are the most similar. In fact, they are thought to hybridize naturally in the wild.

The natural range of the Common Wallaroo includes most regions of Australia including Cape York Peninsula, Central Australia, Hodgson and Victoria. They are found in a variety of habitats including extremely arid regions where annual rainfall is less than 15 inches (380 mm).

Common Wallaroos tend to prefer areas that offer large rocks for shade, though they can also be found in sparsely vegetated areas. This is one of the largest species of wallaroo, with males reaching almost twice the size as females.

At maturity, male Common Wallaroos weigh as much as 78 lbs. (35 kg) while females are just 33 lbs. (15 kg).

Males are 45 to 78 inches (114 to 200 cm) long, with an additional tail length of 21 to 35 inches (53 to 89 cm). Females are 44 to 60 inches (112 to 152 cm) long with a tail length of 21 to 29 inches (53 to 74 inches).

Common Wallaroos have darker, less dense fur than other macropods. The ventral side is typically dark grey with white, sparse fur on the underside. Their bare noses are black, with equally dark coloration at the back of the ears.

The lips, base, and inside of the ears, however, are pale or white. The legs and tail vary slightly in color from the body, being dark brown and bleeding to black near the tips.

Common Wallaroos are opportunistic breeders and generally do not exhibit any kind of seasonal pattern for mating.

Females reach sexual maturity at around 18 months while males may not be fully mature until 22 months of age.

When conditions are good, females often have one joey attached to the teat and another either in the pouch or out of the pouch but still nursing.

The gestation period is about 34 days, and the time a joey spends in the pouch ranges from 237 to 269 days.

The average lifespan of the Common Wallaroo in the wild is 18.5 years, while the captive lifespan can be a whole year longer. The key to their longevity is the fact that these wallaroos are well adapted to survival in dry environments.

In their native habitat, temperatures can exceed 120°F (49°C) but Common Wallaroos have several means of thermo-regulating their bodies to survive. In excessive heat, they pant. They may also dig a hole in the ground to keep cool.

b.) Black Wallaroo (*Macropus bernardus*)

The Black Wallaroo is found within a limited area on the western edge of Arnhem Land, in northern Australia. They are typically found in closed forests, Eucalyptus forests, or open grasslands. They tend to prefer habitats with large boulders to provide cover.

Males are generally sooty brown or black in color while females are dark brown or grey. Black Wallaroos are the smallest species of wallaroo and the smallest in the kangaroo family.

These animals range in size from 28 to 48 lbs. (13 to 22 kg) and have a have a length from 2.6 to 3.3 feet (0.8 to 1 meter). Black Wallaroo about 2/3 the size of Common Wallaroos, and have shorter ears.

Black Wallaroos can breed throughout the year as long as conditions remain optimal. Gestation lasts between 31-36 days with the young remaining exclusively in the pouch for about 4 months.

Though all wallaroos tend to be somewhat solitary, the Black Wallaroo is rarely found in groups consisting of more than three individuals. These groups often include a male, a female and a large joey.

When two males encounter each other, they may exhibit aggressive behavior, walking stiff legged, pulling on grass, or straining to exaggerate their height. These confrontations tend to end quickly and generally do not lead to injury.

Black Wallaroos are one of the least studied species in the kangaroo family because they are incredibly shy. When approached, they tend to flee until they are out of eyesight.

What is known about this species is that they spend 7 to 14 hours a day grazing and are most active at dawn and at dusk. They use camouflage to hide from predators including eagles, dingoes, crocodiles, foxes, and humans.

There are currently several conservation efforts in place to preserve the Black Wallaroo species. A large part of their natural habitat is located in Kakadu National Park in Australia, which is already protected.

c.) Antilopine Wallaroo (*Macropus antilopinus*)

The Antilopine Wallaroo lives in the savanna woodlands in the northern and tropical regions of Australia. Their native habitat ranges from Kimberley to the Gulf of Carpentaria, though they are also found in the Cape York Peninsula.

These wallaroos spend their days resting in shaded areas, coming out at dusk to graze. During the wet season, they may also graze during the day when the weather is cool, but will return to shelter during periods of heavy rain.

Antilopine Wallaroos are one of the most sexually dimorphic of the wallaroo species. Males exhibit a reddish tan color while females are brown with grey heads and shoulders. Females also have white tips on the back of their ears.

Both sexes have white feet and paws tipped in black. Males have a swelling above their nostrils which is believed to help keep them cool.

In terms of size, male Antilopine Wallaroos can reach up to 150 lbs. (70 kg) while females range from 30-65 lbs. (15-30 kg). The average length is 5-6 ft. (1.5-1.9 m).

Though little information is available regarding the lifespan of the Antilopine Wallaroo in the wild, the longest recorded survival in captivity is 16 years.

Unlike other species, the Antilopine Wallaroo breeds once per year, generally starting in December near the beginning of the wet season.

While females of the species become sexually mature around 16 months (and develop their pouch after 20 months), males do not mature for closer to 2 years.

Once conception occurs, the gestation period lasts about 35 days. Only one joey is born per breeding season and it develops inside the pouch for about 20 weeks.

After 6 months, the joey emerges, but continues to nurse until about 15 months of age. Once the joey reaches the mother's pouch, the males lose interest and join male-only groups. Females remain together with their young.

Antilopine Wallaroos are more social than other species. Joeys tend to stay near their mothers even into adulthood, resting together and grooming each other.

Older males are more solitary, but younger males often form "bachelor groups," while females form larger groups with their young. These groups move annually between regular grazing grounds.

4) What About The Kangaroo?

The kangaroo is the largest species in the *Macropodidae* family and it is endemic to Australia. The kangaroo appears on the national coat of arms, and on some of the currency.

Its likeness is rife in popular culture, and is the "image" of all things Australian for the rest of the world.

Keeping kangaroos as pets, however, is a somewhat difficult matter due to their vastly larger size. Wallabies, wallaroos, and kangaroos all have very similar body structure, but some species of kangaroos can reach a maximum weight of 200 lbs. (90 kg).

Kangaroos move by hopping with their powerful hind legs and they are capable of reaching speeds up to 44 mph (70 km/h). When moving at slower speeds, the kangaroo often uses its tail and forelimbs as a tripod, raising its hind legs forward.

You may be surprised to hear that kangaroos are also very good swimmers – they often escape into the water when pursued by predators.

Kangaroo have a chambered stomach like that of a cow or sheep. In a similar way to livestock, they regurgitate food that has already been consumed and continue to chew it, breaking it down further for easier digestion.

This action, known as "chewing their cud," helps to give kangaroos their oddly matter-of-fact expression. It's quite common for a roo to stand up and stare with a rather benign, bored look that only compliments its whimsical charm.

All kangaroos are herbivores, though some subsist exclusively on grasses while others also eat some shrubs. If you do not have a rural setting for them to graze and range, they are extremely difficult pets to keep.

Certainly wallabies and wallaroos after one year of age do not qualify as house pets, but their smaller size makes them more manageable as companions than their larger cousins.

Ch. 2) - What to Know Before You Buy

Wallabies and wallaroos are not typical household pets. These animals have a variety of specific needs in regard to housing and diet.

Before you go out and purchase either species, you must be certain that you can provide an appropriate home, and that you understand the pros and cons of becoming a macropod owner .

1.) Do You Need a License?

Both wallabies and wallaroos are considered exotic animals and may be subject to laws governing their import, export, and keeping.

It is imperative that you research all potential legal ramifications before your purchase your pet. Failure to do so will not only subject you to fines, but may result in the seizure of the unfortunate and innocent animal.

a.) Licensing in the U.S.

In the United States, the definition of the term "exotic" is ever-changing. Traditionally, "exotic" refers to an animal that is neither native nor indigenous to the owner's locale. Legally, however, the term may be defined differently from one jurisdiction to another.

The federal government defines an exotic animal as "an animal that is native to a foreign country or of foreign origin or character, is not native to the United States, or was introduced from abroad."

Licensing requirements vary greatly from one state to another. Many states have laws forbidding the possession of exotic animals, while others simply require a license – some have no licensing or permit requirements at all.

Overview of State Exotic Animal Laws:

At the time of this writing, late in 2013, the following information regarding state law in the United States was accurate. Be advised, however, that the language of these statutes is often convoluted and confusing. It is always best to verify the legal status of any exotic animal BEFORE you purchase your pet.

Most Dangerous Captive Wildlife Banned as Pets

California
Colorado
Georgia
Illinois
Iowa
Kentucky
New Mexico
New Hampshire
New York
New Jersey
Maryland
Oregon
Washington
Utah

Bans Some Species but Allows Others

Arkansas
Kansas
Florida
Maine
Louisiana
Michigan
Minnesota
Montana
Nebraska
Wyoming
Tennessee

Doesn't Ban Captive Wildlife, Requires Permit for Some

Arizona
Idaho
North Dakota
South Dakota
Oklahoma
Texas
Missouri
Mississippi
Indiana
Pennsylvania
Virginia
Rhode Island

No Regulation or Restriction on Captive Wildlife

Nevada
Wisconsin
Ohio
West Virginia
North Carolina
South Carolina

b.) Licensing in the U.K.

In 1976, the Dangerous Wild Animals Act was enacted in the United Kingdom. This act was passed in reaction to the increasing number of people seeking to keep exotic pets, which tend to be more dangerous than the traditional domestic cat or dog.

The act was also designed to regulate the keeping of hybrids between wild and domestic species. Though neither wallabies nor wallaroos are typically dangerous to humans, they are still considered wild animals and their export, import and keeping is strictly regulated.

Some of the animals specified as "dangerous" by the act include primates, carnivores, large reptiles, spiders and scorpions.

Several species of marsupial, including wallaroos are also included in this list, although in most cases wallabies are allowed.

In order to legally keep these animals in the UK, you must apply for a license and pay a fee. The information on the license and the regulations set forth may vary slightly from one region to another, so be sure to contact your local council regarding specific requirements in your area.

For a full text version of the Dangerous Wild Animals Act 1976, visit: www.legislation.gov.uk/ukpga/1976/38

2.) How Many Should You Buy?

The number of macropods you purchase to keep as pets depends on a variety of factors, the single most important being space. Wallabies and wallaroos are active wild animals in need of adequate exercise. They do not do well when confined to close quarters.

When thinking about multiple macropods, consider both size and personality. Some species are more social than others.

Generally, it is not a good idea to keep a pair of males together unless you have multiple females as well. Your best bet, if you plan to keep more than one macropod, is to keep several small females or several females along with their young.

Keep in mind that as your wallabies or wallaroos grow, you may need to reduce the number you keep or increase the amount of space you use for their enclosure. As young joeys mature, they may come into competition with each other if they are male.

There is no specific formula for keeping multiple macropods together – it largely depends on the socialization and the individual temperaments of the animals.

If you plan to keep more than one macropod in the same enclosure, make sure the area is large enough that each animal has its own space. Carefully observe the animals at all times to make sure they are getting along.

3.) Can Macropods Be Kept with Other Pets?

The answer to this question varies from one animal to another depending on the wallaby or wallaroo's temperament. Some smaller wallabies may see other pets like dogs and large cats as threats, while larger wallaroos may have no trouble getting along with Fido and Fluffy.

It is best to keep young joeys away from other pets but adults can be compatible with domesticated animals as long as you supervise their interaction.

It is never a good idea to leave your macropods alone with other pets because you never know how the animals will react to one another – it is always better to be safe than sorry.

Young joeys could be severely injured by a family dog that is simply over-excited. Wallabies, wallaroos, and kangaroos should NOT be kept with cats.

The macropods can become infected with the protozoan that causes toxoplasmosis, which may be present in the feces of cats even if the cat itself shows no symptoms. This disease is fatal to joeys of all macropod species.

4.) Ease and Cost of Care

Because of their energy and overall friendly natures, both wallabies and wallaroos are a pleasure to keep as pets, especially when they have been bottle raised. That bonding experience makes them unusually affectionate and loyal with their humans.

Before you purchase a macropod, take the time to make sure that you are able to cover all of the initial costs of purchasing your pet as well as the monthly costs you can expect to pay over the lifetime.

a.) Initial Costs

The initial costs for keeping a wallaby or wallaroo will include the actual cost of the animal as well as the necessary accessories and veterinary procedures.

Purchase Price - Prices for both wallabies and wallaroos vary greatly depending where you purchase them. Because both are still fairly rare as pets, there aren't a large number of breeders and prices are quite high – usually between $1,000 and $4,000 (£646 to £2585).

Microchipping - It is not a requirement that you have your macropod microchipped, but it is definitely a good idea. In the event that your wallaby or wallaroo gets lost, you stand a much higher chance of being reunited with him if it has been microchipped. The average cost for this service is around $40 (£30).

Vaccinations - If you purchase a macropod from a reputable breeder, it should already be up to date on its vaccinations.

If it is not, or if you purchase an older animal, you should take it to the veterinarian to have it vaccinated. The cost for this service may vary between $50 and $100 (£37 to £75).

Food/Water Containers - In order to feed macropods, you will need a free standing or wall mounted hay rack as well as a dry trough for food. Additionally, you will need several containers for fresh water.

The cost for these items may range from $100 to $150 (£65 - £97). Don't neglect to factor in multiple feeders if you have more than one pet, or if you are providing both indoor and outdoor feeding options.

Enclosure - The cost of your macropod enclosure will depend on a number of factors including size, quality of materials, type of bedding, and included furnishings.

The range for enclosure costs falls between $500 and $2000 (£323 - £1293). Depending on climate, you may be looking at a pen with "lean to" like sleeping accommodations, or a pen with an actual shed or small barn.

Be advised that groups of macropods will sleep together, so all shelters will need to be large enough for all of your pets to bed down together in one big bunch.

Wallabies and wallaroos take rather well to creature comforts, and enjoy large, soft dog beds, which you can scatter around their primary pen or inside their shed.

It's difficult to put an exact cost estimate on your enclosure since there are so many variables. If you are a do-it-yourself type, you can save a great deal of money on both labor and materials. I recommend going online and looking at photos of wallaby and wallaroo enclosures to get ideas for design and arrangement.

Summary of Initial Costs

Cost Type	One Pet	Two Pets
Purchase Price	$1,000 to $4,000 (£646 to £2585)	$2,000 to $8,000 (£1293 to £5171)
Microchipping	$40 (£30)	$80 (£60)
Vaccinations	$50 - $100 (£37 - £75)	$100 - $200 (£75 - £150)
Food/Water Containers	$100 - $150 (£65 - £97)	$200 - $300 (£120 - £194)
Enclosure	$500 and $2,000 (£323 - £1293)	$500 and $2,000 (£323 - £1293)
Total:	$1,690 - $6,140 (£1,092 - £3,968)	$2,880 - $10,580 (£1,861 - £6,838)

b.) Monthly Costs

The monthly costs for keeping a macropod may vary depending on whether you have one or more, the type of food used, and the preferred bedding.

Food - The most important cost you will face on a monthly basis is food. This amount will vary depending on type and quality. For one wallaby or wallaroo, you can expect to pay about $200 to $400 (£123 - £246) per month.

The following products are meant as examples of the types of food you will use with your pets. Please note that prices will differ by locality and availability.

If you feed horse or "pony" cubes, you'll pay, on average $45-$50 / £25-£31 for 88 lbs. / 40 kgs.

Prices per bale of alfalfa hay will vary by location and amount. It is important that the hay be dry and fresh. If you buy by the bale, expect to pay $225 / £8 per ton (2000 lbs./907 kg).

Kangaroo muesli or mixed food, which is fine for wallabies and wallaroos is priced at $45 / £28 per 77 lbs. / 35 kgs.

Vaccinations - To protect your pet from disease, you should administer vaccines based on your veterinarian's recommendations. Vaccinations typically cost around $10 (£7.50) per injection.

Veterinary Check-Ups – Typically only an annual visit to the vet will be required. The total cost for this visit should be under $50 (£37.40), which averages to about $4.16 (£3) per month.

Other Costs - Be prepared to cover some extra costs once in a while like replacing enclosure furnishings, cage repairs and other things you may have to purchase on occasion.

The average monthly cost for these extra items is around $10 (£7.5).

Summary of Monthly Costs

Cost Type	One Pet	Two Pets
Food	$200 to $400 (£123 - £246)	$400 to $600 (£246 - £369)
Vaccinations	$10 (£7.50)	$20 (£15)
Veterinary Check-Ups	$4.16 (£3)	$8 (£6)
Other Costs	$10 (£7.5)	$10 (£7.5)
Total:	$224 - $448 (£137 - £274)	$438 - $638 (£154 - £283)

Pros and Cons of Owning a Wallaby or Wallaroo

One of the major draws of keeping either a wallaby or a wallaroo as a pet is their exotic nature. At the same time, however, that can be considered a drawback.

Pros of Wallabies and Wallaroos as Pets

- If properly socialized, can be very friendly
- Can be trained to follow simple commands
- Commercial diets are available for easy feeding
- Are often very affectionate with humans, form strong bonds
- Unique pets, always entertaining to have around
- Joeys can be hand-raised on formula
- Very gentle by nature, especially if properly socialized around humans

Cons of Wallabies and Wallaroos as Pets

- Depending on species, can grow fairly large
- Can become mischievous, may do some damage if not properly supervised
- Require a significant amount of space – a fenced pen or pasture is necessary
- Can be very expensive to purchase and keep compared to other pets
- Some species are nocturnal, may not be very active during the day

Ch. 3) - Purchasing Wallabies and Wallaroos

Purchasing a wallaby or a wallaroo is not as easy as going to your local pet store. You may not be able to find a breeder in your immediate area.

If this is the case, I strongly advise against having a joey shipped to you. It would be far preferable for you to drive to the breeding establishment to pick up the animal.

Young joeys are shy and sensitive by nature. They are extremely susceptible to changes in temperature and humidity, and crave the feeling of security that comes with growing up in their mother's pouch.

For these and other reasons, many breeders will not even consider shipping the animals, so you may need to factor travel costs into your initial purchase expense.

1.) Buying in the U.S.

In the United States, in order to obtain legal animals that have been raised in good circumstances, contact dealers online.

One of the best providers of wallaroos in the U.S. is Schreiner Farms of Dallesport, Washington. (The ranch also breeds and sells cattle, ostrich, camel, zebra, and other exotic animals.)

Schreiner Farms
www.schreinerfarms.com

Buffalo Hill Exotics in Centralia, Illinois raises both Bennett's and Dama wallabies in addition to miniature horses, red kangaroos, miniature zebra, cattle, buffalo, Bactrian camels, and miniature long-haired dachshunds.

Buffalo Hill Exotics
www.buffalohillexotics.com

Valley Stables Exotics of Berea, Kentucky offers Bennett's Wallabies in addition to African Serval Cats, African Caracal Lynx, miniature llamas, and a range of other animals.

Valley Stables Exotics
www.valleystables-exotics.com

The Fall City Wallaby Ranch located in Fall City, Washington also offers Red Kangaroos in addition to Grey and Albino Bennett's Wallabies.

Fall City Wallaby Ranch
www.wallabyranch.org

2.) Buying in the U.K.

Because the keeping of wallaroos and potentially wallabies is heavily regulated in the U.K. it may be tricky to find one for purchase. To begin your search try:

Wallabies and Wabbits
www.wallabiesandwabbits.co.uk

3.) How to Select a Healthy Wallaroo

The last thing you want is to go through the trouble to find a quality macropod breeder only to bring your pet home and discover it is suffering from a health problem.

Some of the things to look for in a healthy macropod:

- Eyes are bright and alert
- No visible signs of injury or illness
- Fluid movements, not limping or dragging limbs
- Even temperament, seems well socialized

- Not afraid of humans
- No discharge from the eyes, nose or mouth
- Healthy appetite, not refusing food
- No signs of diarrhea in the pen
- Coat is in good condition, not rough or patchy

Ch. 4) - Caring for Wallabies and Wallaroos

In order to keep your wallabies and wallaroos healthy and happy there are two things you need to be mindful about – diet and habitat. If both are well designed to meet your macropod's basic needs, there is no reason why your pet shouldn't thrive.

1.) First Year of Life

Typically when you purchase a joey from a breeder you will be provided with a pouch, a bottle with appropriate marsupial nipples, an initial container of milk supplement, and a package of information about nurturing the baby.

To purchase milk replacement products and nursing supplies on your own, please see:

Wombaroo.com / Perfect Pets Inc.
www.perfectpet.net/wombaroo/index.html
23180 Sherwood Rd.
Belleville, MI 48111
1-800-366-8794

Please note that this company will ship internationally.

Due to the exotic nature of the species, most breeders are prepared to be your "go to" source of information on what the joey will need to thrive.

You can liken raising a joey to having a newborn infant in the house. The baby should spend as much time with you in its pouch as possible. Joeys are happiest when you simply wear the pouch and truly act as a surrogate mother.

This will not only give the little one a sense of security, but it's an excellent bonding experience. Bottle fed joeys grow up to be extremely affectionate and loyal, far over and above the expectations most people have for them. They are excellent pets!

If you are in a situation of raising an orphaned joey, you can use an old blanket as a substitute pouch, or any material that is soft and washable.

Commercially designed pouches retail for $20-$50 / £12-£30.

The pouch should be large enough for the baby to have plenty of room to move around, but also to feel snug. When you are not wearing the pouch, it should always be suspended and the bottom should not be allowed to touch the floor.

You do, however, want to keep the pouch near enough to the floor that the joey can jump out on its own without fear of injury.

a.) Regulating Temperature

Joeys have no way to regulate their own body temperature. The baby will rely on you to make sure it stays warm. In the wild, joeys don't leave the pouch until they have a good layer of fur on their bodies. The interior of the mother's pouch stays around 86-90 F / 30-32 C.

In captivity, a small heating pad outside the pouch works well to ensure that the joey stays warm. Wombaroo sells a "Cosy Heat Pad" measuring 102" x 14.2" / 260mm x 360mm that has been designed particularly for use with orphaned marsupials.

The unit retails for approximately $89 / £55.

The surface of the pad reaches a temperature of 59-68 F / 15-20 C above the ambient room temperature. Adjust the amount of heat the joey receives by increasing or decreasing intervening layers of material placed between the pad and the pouch.

Carefully monitor the temperature inside the pouch with a thermometer and do not allow the baby to overheat. Heat stress can easily be fatal to a joey.

b.) Feeding a Joey

Note that if you have not been supplied with a proper bottle and marsupial teat from a breeder, you will need to acquire this equipment as soon as possible.

Joeys have very tender mouths and cannot use hard rubber teats. A special marsupial nipple will be required. These nipples vary in size and cost less than $2 / £1.22 each.

A mother macropod's milk changes composition over the course of the joey's development to supply the correct nutritional levels. Milk replacement products for joeys are therefore rated by age in an effort to match these growth patterns.

Manufacturers like Wombaroo Food Products compile growth charts to aid surrogate joey parents in selecting the right grade of food and the correct feeding amounts. The food comes packaged as a dry powder to be mixed with water.

Always feed your joey in the pouch, then remove the animal and take it to the toilet. The baby's mother would simulate urination and defecation by licking. Simply tap or gently stroke the joey's anal area with a tissue or damp washcloth to replicate this action.

Joeys should be toileted after feedings and when they wake up from a nap. This is an extremely important aspect of hand rearing since the animals will be subject to urinary tract and bowel diseases if they are not toileted frequently enough.

If your joey was obtained from a breeder, the animal should be quite comfortable taking a bottle. If, however, you are raising an orphan, the baby may have to get used to the process.

Gently cup your hand under the baby's chin and cover its eyes to help the animal quieten down enough to start eating.

Follow the frequency of feeding recommended on the supplemental product you are using until the baby is ready for solid foods.

Most breeders suggest that joeys be allowed to take a bottle as long as they like. In time, the joey will refuse a liquid diet and it will be time to transition to adult foods.

When the joey begins to lose interest in the bottle, you can begin to offer it little bits of green grass before serving the typically recommended diet of hay and cubed foods.

c.) Introducing Solid Food to Joeys

Though macropod joeys may nurse for up to 14 months, they will eat more and more solid food as they grow and mature.

While joeys are still young, their digestive systems are monogastic – a simple type of digestive system similar to that of humans. As the baby matures, however, it becomes dependent upon bacteria to ferment the food it consumes in the stomach.

In order for this process to be successful, the bacteria must become established. This can be difficult for hand-raised joeys without contact with the mother or other adult macropods.
It is not uncommon for joeys to begin nibbling solid food at a fairly early age. You should encourage them to do so by

placing small pieces of native plants in their pouch where they will find it.

If you live in an area where you have access to wild native plants, be sure to pick them from safe sources, not from the roadside where they may be contaminated with pesticides. Once your joey starts to show more interest in solid food you can introduce it to an adult feed.

The feed you offer young joeys should be made up of equal parts of alfalfa hay (Lucerne chaff), kangaroo muesli (available commercially), and kangaroo cubes (or pony cubes sometimes referred to as "cake.")

While feeding your joey this mixture, continue to offer native vegetation but do not start to give the baby apples or green grass yet.

It is important to wait until your joey is used to a solid food diet and that he has begun to expel adult pellets – this is the sign that his body is ready to accept adult foods.

d.) Using a Playpen

During the first year of the joey's life when your pet is not directly under your supervision, the use of a child's mesh playpen is highly recommended. This gives the joey a place to safely get in and out of its pouch while keeping the little fellow from getting into too much trouble.

2.) Habitat Requirements

Even with the smaller wallabies, an outside enclosure for your macropod will become necessary after about a year. The habitat should be as natural as possible. It should also be predator-proof, escape-proof, and comfortable for your pet.

The rule of thumb to follow when it comes to creating a habitat is "bigger is better." The ideal habitat for a wallaby or wallaroo is a large fenced-in pen or pasture where the animals have room to roam.

If you live in an area where large predators are common, you may want to consider placing a border of electric fencing outside the fence of your wallaroo enclosure. It's important, however, that this barrier be beyond the fencing your pets can reach.

Although macropods are known for their jumping ability, these animals are much more likely to try to go through a fence than over it, so be careful not to create any "safety" precautions that will only wind up harming your pet.

If your pet does crash headlong into a fence, seek veterinary assistance immediately as the animal will likely suffer a serious neck injury.

a.) Tips for Fencing Enclosures

Fencing is an incredibly important aspect of your enclosure because it ensures that your macropods can't get out and predators cannot get in.

Ideally, the fence should be at least 6.5 feet (2 m) tall with 1.5 feet (0.5 m) of fencing buried to prevent dogs, foxes, and similar predators from digging their way underneath.

You should also have the top 1.5 feet (0.5 m) of the fence hanging out away from the enclosure at a 45-degree angle. If you are using wire mesh for your fencing, be sure the spacing is small enough that your wallabies and wallaroos cannot get their heads stuck.

Do not underestimate either species' level of curiosity. Do not allow gaps in the fencing that will attract their attention. They will "check out" these spaces, and they will get themselves into trouble.

Plan the fence lines to avoid having large trees too close to the border. A frightened macropod could collide with the tree trunk in a panic and seriously injure himself.

You should also consider planting bushes (if they are not there already) in the corners of the enclosure for the safety of your pets.

If you are using large posts to support wire or chain link fencing, be sure to position the posts outside the enclosure.

You want to make sure the animals can't get their limbs or digits caught between the post and the netting.

b.) Constructing Holding Areas

In addition to the enclosure itself, you also need to build several holding yards. These yards should be connected to the main enclosure by a gate, but should also be able to be closed off entirely.

A smaller holding area will come in handy when you need to provide your pets with medical attention or if you are introducing a new macropod to the group.

To reduce stress, you might also want to consider installing visual barriers such as shade cloth to give your wallabies and wallaroos a feeling of security when they are in the holding area.

c.) Habitat Details

The recommendations in this section are based on the spatial requirements set forth by the Exhibiting Animals Protection Act of 1981 for Australian mammals.

The minimum enclosure area for two macropods is 820 feet^2 (250 m^2). For each additional animal, you will need to add 18 feet^2 (5.50 m^2).

Keep in mind that these requirement are a minimum – it is always better to provide your pets with a little bit of extra space if you can.

Provide your macropods with two open-fronted shelters in each yard. One should face north and another should face south to provide maximum protection during inclement weather.

Depending on your climate, you will need to provide your macropods with either a lean-to shelter or an actual heated barn.

Plan on one large enclosure for all your animals rather than individual shelter. Multiple animals will choose to sleep together.

d.) Furnishing the Enclosure

Choose a substrate for the enclosure that compacts easily by is soft on the animal's feet. Bare concrete should never be used. Grassy yards are the preferred option, planted with a mixture of summer and winter grasses.

You shouldn't be afraid to leave some fallen leaves in place, especially under shade trees, because wallabies and wallaroos like to dig into these areas for a cool place to lie down.

In short-term situations, you can use rubber matting over concrete but, again, this is not the ideal long-term solution.

Logs and leafy branches are the ideal forms of decoration. Rough-barked trees will provide enrichment as well as a source of roughage.

You may also want to think about adding piles of logs, hard plastic cylinders, and other installations to provide recreation. Fast-growing native shrubs and bushes are also a great addition.

3.) Feeding Wallaroos

Wallabies and wallaroos are herbivores by nature, which means that they subsist entirely on plants. The major portion of their diet is made up of grass, though some also eat shrubs and herbs.

Most species are grazing animals, moving a short distance away from shelter during the cooler parts of the day to find food. They generally return to shelter when it gets hot.

Wallabies and wallaroos can survive for long periods of time without drinking water, as long as they receive hydration from the plants they eat.

a.) Types of Food

As your pet ages you can begin to introduce him to other foods. Wallabies and wallaroos should always have access to fresh water. Some of the foods your Wallaroo may enjoy include:

- Rolled oats
- Horse stud mix
- Natural (unsweetened) muesli
- Soft Lucerne hay
- Grass (with roots attached)
- Horse pellets
- Dairy meal
- Carrots and celery
- Sweet potato
- Apples

**Note: Keep in mind that when feeding grains, they should always be crushed. Also, never feed fresh alfalfa, Lucerne, or clover – only hay is recommended.

b.) Captive vs. Wild Feeding of Adults

In the wild, wallabies and wallaroos are grazers – they feed largely on grass, but some species also eat shrubs. In captivity, the diet is not significantly different. It is based on a foundation of hay and grass supplemented with commercial pellets or cubes.

The grazing styles of wild wallabies and wallaroos vary from one season to the next, depending on the availability of food.

c.) Foods and Supplements

Commercial pellets or cubes are an important part of a captive macropod's diet because they contain some of the nutrients these animals need that can't be found in grass. The typical nutritional analysis of commercial pellets is as follows:

- Crude protein, min. 14.0%
- Crude fat, min. 3.0%
- Crude fiber, max. 13.0%
- Actual salt 0.75%
- Fluorine, max. 0.0096%

Lucerne or alfalfa hay is the staple of a macropod's diet. This type of hay is high in dietary fiber which is important for animals that have fermentation chambers as part of their digestive system.

You should be aware that alfalfa or Lucerne chaff can have sharp pieces. Don't be tempted to purchase low-quality feed that can injure your pet's gums.

d.) Presentation of Food

Clean containers are the most crucial aspect of food presentation. The best containers are sturdy plastic or aluminum trays that prevent the food from spoiling but allow easy access.

Select water containers with enough room for your pets to immerse their forelegs if they want to cool down.

A pellet bin or trough is a good choice along with hay racks to prevent food from becoming soiled.

Using a high-quality feeder will prevent the food from being dragged out over the ground and will also ensure that all animals present have access to the food, even those that have a lower ranking in the social group.

Ch. 5) - Breeding Wallabies and Wallaroos

Breeding wallabies and wallaroos can be very challenging but it is not impossible if you have all of the necessary information at hand.

In this chapter you will find basic breeding information as well as tips for hand raising joeys.

1.) Basic Breeding Info

Male macropods can have multiple female partners at one time. Unlike some animals, they do not mate for life and they may not even mate with the same female twice.

The estrus cycle of females varies slightly depending on the species and subspecies as does the gestation period for the young. Macropod offspring do not develop in a placenta like other animals.

Immediately after birth, the baby climbs through the mother's fur and into her pouch where it suckles and continues to grow another 230-270 days on average.

Even after emerging from the pouch, joeys may continue to suckle for up to 14 months. Sexual maturity in both wallabies and wallaroos is typically reached in 1-2 years.

Females are capable of becoming pregnant almost immediately after giving birth due to the process of embryonic diapause. The new embryo goes dormant until the existing fetus leaves the pouch.

a) Summary of Breeding Info

Breeding Style: polygynous, opportunistic

Estrus Cycle: varies by species, 32 to 45 days

Gestation Period: varies by species, 30 to 38 days

Development in Pouch: 230 to 270 days

Nursing: 12 to 14 months

Sexual Maturity (female): 14 to 24 months

Sexual Maturity (male): 18 to 20 months

Additional Facts: embryonic diapause allows female to become pregnant again very shortly after birth

2.) Mating and the Birthing Process

The details of the breeding process are not well known for all species due of wallabies and wallaroos to the often difficult proposition of observing natural mating behavior in the wild.

In general, female macropods are entirely passive during mating while the male becomes solely focused on the act. Once conception occurs, females go through a period of gestation that lasts between 30 and 38 days.

In the hours preceding the birth, the female spends several hours cleaning her abdomen and pouch, licking a trail in her fur leading up to the pouch.

While preparing to give birth, the female often uses a vertical object to support herself as the contractions begin.

After enduring periodic contractions, the female gives birth to a wriggling neonate, still attached to the umbilical cord. After birth, the female moves into a sitting position at which point the neonate begins to climb toward the pouch.

After 8 to 10 minutes, the neonate makes its way into the pouch where it attaches to the teat and remains there for between 4 and 6 months.

Though the exact time may vary depending on the species, joeys typically emerge from the pouch after about 6 months. For the next several weeks, the joey spends time both in and outside the pouch, learning to hop and growing quickly.

After about 37 weeks, the female stops allowing the joey to return to the pouch. At this point, the joey will continue to nurse by putting its head inside the pouch for another 3 to 5 months. It will most likely be weaned by the age of 14 months.

3.) Raising the Babies

In the wild, joeys nurse from their mothers until they are 12 to 14 months of age. If you are breeding your own macropods or buying a wallaby or wallaroo joey, you may be faced with hand-rearing the infant.

Some of the supplies you will require include:

- Natural fiber (wool or cotton) pouch
- 100 ml bottle with macropod teats
- Thermometer
- Hot water bottle
- Pillow cases or blankets
- Sterilizing solution

The most important thing you need to know about bottle-feeding joeys is that fluids should be served at blood temperature.

To prepare the formula, use pre-boiled water that has been cooled. If you use boiling water, it may destroy the mineral content of the formula.

As you are feeding your joey, wrap it carefully in the pouch and use the hot water bottle to keep it warm between 90° and 95°F (32° to 35°C).

Keep in mind that joeys may not take to the bottle right away. It is best to be patient and give your joey plenty of time to get used to the bottle.

Once your joey catches on, nursing can be a wonderful, bonding experience. As your joey feeds, make sure to keep it secure in its pouch on your lap, close to your body.

You may, at first, need to cover the joey's eyes and open its mouth with your thumb to insert the bottle. Eventually the joey will settle down. It is important that you never squeeze the bottle because this could cause the liquid to enter the joey's lungs.

Joeys require a low-lactose diet because they are unable to digest milk with high lactose content. The three formulas recommended for wallaby and wallaroo joeys are DiVetalact, Biolac and Wombaroo which can be purchased online.

Follow the directions on the package strictly to avoid making the formula stronger than your joey can tolerate.

Formula should never be reheated and, once mixed, should always be stored in the refrigerator. Bottles and teats should be washed after every use and any milk spilt from the joey's mouth should be wiped up immediately.

Ch. 6) - Healthy Wallabies and Wallaroos

In order to keep your wallabies and wallaroos safe and healthy, it is important that you learn to recognize the symptoms of disease. The more quickly treatment is provided, the greater the chance that the animal will recover successfully.

1.) Common Health Problems

If well fed and kept in clean conditions, wallabies and wallaroos tend to be hardy and healthy animals, although they are somewhat sensitive to stress.

When health issues do arise, the following problems are the ones most typically seen in both species.

a) Hair Loss

Hair loss in macropods can be the result of several different things. The two most common causes, however, are stress and inadequate diet.

In the case of young joeys, an environment that is too warm can also lead to hair loss. Other possible culprits include fungal infection, skin irritation, or bleach present in soap powders used on items with which the animal comes into contact.

The treatment for hair loss varies depending on the cause. Fungal infections can be treated with topical creams.

Reducing stress levels may require you to evaluate your pet's living situation and to make adjustments where needed.

Causes: stress, fungal infection, inadequate diet, skin irritation, etc.

Symptoms: bald patches, loss of hair over large areas

Treatment: anti-fungal cream for fungal infections, improved diet, evaluation of living situation

b) Fleas

In most cases, wallabies and wallaroos catch fleas through contact with other domestic animals including dogs and cats.

Your macropods may also contract lice. The treatment for both parasites is identical: carboryl or pyrethrum-based powder.

You should also take steps to avoid re-infestation by treating other pets with anti-flea medications.

Causes: contact with other domestic animals

Symptoms: itching, irritation, redness of skin

Treatment: carboryl or pyrethrum-based powder

c) Ticks

Ticks can be very dangerous for wallabies and wallaroos because they attach to the skin and gorge themselves on the animal's blood.

If a macropod has too many ticks, it can suffer from blood loss or anemia. When the parasites first attach, ticks often look like brown seeds with legs. As they feed, however, they grow larger and often taken on an off-white color.

Once the tick has fed sufficiently it will drop off the animal and multiply on the ground. In order to remove a tick, first coat the parasite with a substance like petroleum jelly.

This will suffocate the tick and allow you to grasp it firmly by the head with a pair of tweezers. The jaws will be relaxed, but do not twist the tick as you pull and be sure not to leave the head embedded.

Causes: attachment/embedding of tick

Symptoms: itching, scratching, visible attachment, anemia

Treatment: suffocate with petroleum jelly, grasp it firmly by the head with a pair of tweezers and pull the head out

d) Bowel Prolapse

In cases of severe diarrhea in macropods, it is not uncommon for the bowel to become prolapsed. This condition involves the exposure of the bowel, which may pop out entirely and need to be pushed back in.

In some cases, the condition will resolve itself with an hour but, in severe cases, your pet may need veterinary care to have a stitch put in to hold the bowel in place.

Causes: severe diarrhea

Symptoms: pain and discomfort, difficult bowel movements, bloody stool, visible prolapse

Treatment: sometimes resolves itself within an hour; may need veterinary care to have a stitch put in to keep the bowel in place

e) Scours

Also known simply as diarrhea, scours is often the result of poor hygiene or improper diet. The condition may also be the result of a bacterial or viral infection in the intestines, however.

In some cases, scours result when the joey is fed too much food or the wrong food, which cannot be digested properly.

Treatment of this condition should be determined by a veterinarian, but generally involves medication and the administration of electrolytes or probiotics.

Causes: often the result of poor hygiene or improper diet

Symptoms: diarrhea, liquid stools, frequent defecation

Treatment: generally involves medication and the administration of electrolytes or pro-biotics

f) Thrush

Thrush is a type of yeast invasion caused by *Candida Albicans*. This infection can be diagnosed by a gram stain performed by a veterinarian.

Some of the initial symptoms of this disease include diarrhea, a foul smell, and yellowish/green stools or frothy stools.

As the disease progresses, mouth sores and lesions may also appear. The causes of thrush may include stress, poor hygiene, oral antibiotics, or cloaca sucking.

Treatment is generally a 0.1 ml per 1 kg / 2.2 lbs. body weight dose of Nilstat.

Be aware, however, that it is possible for Nilstat to cause diarrhea for the first three to five days so it is important that you offer it between feedings, never in the milk itself, or your joey may not get the nutrition he needs.

Causes: *Candida Albicans*; stress, poor hygiene, oral antibiotics or cloaca sucking

Symptoms: diarrhea, a foul smell, yellowish/green stools or frothy stools; mouth sores and lesions may appear as disease progresses

Treatment: a 0.1 ml per 1 kg body weight dose of Nilstat

g) Pneumonia

There are two main causes of pneumonia in macropods – lack of warmth or inhalation of fluid into the lungs. Both are more common in joeys, especially during feeding.

Hand-raised joeys may be susceptible to inhaling fluid into the lungs if the holes in the teats are too large or if the bottle is squeezed during feeding.

Some of the symptoms of pneumonia include congestion in the chest, sniffling after feeding, listlessness and refusing to eat.

The treatment for pneumonia may depend on the severity of the case. In most cases, antibiotics are recommended. Do not ignore symptoms of respiratory distress in your pet as pneumonia can be life threatening.

The most common antibiotic administered for pneumonia and other respiratory infections is Baytril at a dose of 1 mg per 10 kg / 22 lbs.body weight.

In severe cases, the antibiotic may also be injected into the skin or muscle.

Causes: lack of warmth or inhalation of fluid into the lungs

Symptoms: congestion in the chest, sniffling after feeding, listlessness and refusing to eat

Treatment: antibiotics like Baytril are recommended

h) Necrobacillosis (Lumpy Jaw)

Also called Lumpy Jaw, necrobacillosis is caused by *Fusobacterium necrophorum* and involves necrotizing inflammation of the bone or soft tissues, which may be exacerbated by concurrent infections.

These bacteria are present on the ground, but can only enter the body when the skin is broken. The disease is called Lumpy Jaw because it often affects the jaws of captive macropods.

Unfortunately, infected animals do not always show warning signs until just before death. Some symptoms include lesions and ulcerations, which are often accompanied by a yellow-green pus with a foul odor.

Veterinary care is required to treat this disease. In some cases, the vaccine given to sheep to prevent foot rot has been an effective treatment.

Causes: *Fusobacterium necrophorum*

Symptoms: lesions and ulcerations which are often accompanied by a yellow-green pus with a foul odor

Treatment: veterinary care required; vaccine given to sheep to prevent foot rot may be effective

2.) Diagnosing Injuries

Because your macropods are likely to live outdoors, they are prone to developing injuries at some point. Close observation on your part will prevent minor wounds from turning into major problems.

In many cases, your pet may not make it evident that he is injured. You should be alert for the following signs that something is not right:

- Change in posture or carriage
- Frightened or nervous disposition
- Lethargic or listless
- Limbs hanging loose
- Head or ears hanging down
- Uncoordinated movements, stumbling
- Convulsions or shaking fits
- Deteriorating condition of fur
- Coughing, sneezing, vomiting
- Blood visible on the animal or in the pen
- Change in consistency or color of feces

If you identify any of these signs, you should carefully examine your pet to locate the injury. In order to avoid frightening the animal:

- Perform the examination in a safe area
- Keep all noise to a minimum
- Have all of your tools at-hand so you don't have to leave the animal alone
- Use a system for the examination, start on one side and move toward the other
- Compare both sides of the body to identify changes/injuries
- Stop the examination if your pet becomes stressed or goes into shock

Some of the most common signs of stress include:

- Extreme increase or decrease in activity level
- Attempted escape
- Thumping the ground with feet or tail
- Barking or hissing, grinding teeth
- Head shaking or ear flicking
- Change in body temperature
- Licking forearms, chest or shoulders
- Clawing at itself
- Diarrhea, especially in joeys
- Decreased food intake, failure to thrive

3.) Macropod First Aid

The basic principles of first aid for macropods are the same as they are for humans. Your priorities should be:

1. Safety of the patient
2. Safety of the bystanders
3. Prevention of further injury

The first steps you should take (in order) are:

1. Clearing the airway (if blocked)
2. Stopping the bleeding
3. Maintaining body temperature
4. Minimizing stress

Only after these four steps have been taken should you attempt to treat any wounds or fractures. Below you will find an in-depth explanation of how to perform each of these four steps.

a) Clear the Airway.

Carefully remove any obstructions from the mouth without compromising your own safety. If you aren't able to remove the obstruction yourself, seek immediate veterinary care.

If your pet doesn't have an obstruction to his breathing, simply place him in a warm, safe area and observe him. In cases where your macropod loses consciousness, lay him on his side with his head lowered (but still above stomach level).

This will keep the larynx open and will allow fluids to drain. You should also check to be sure that the nostrils are clear of debris.

b) Stop the Bleeding.

To stop the bleeding of an open wound, apply firm pressure with your hands or with a bandage.

If the animal is struggling, try to keep your pet calm. If it continues to flail, you will have a much more difficult time staunching the bleeding.

If the bleeding continues, use a soft dressing to cover the wound and secure it with a bandage. Seek veterinary assistance as soon as possible.

It is important that you do not let any bandages obstruct your pet's breathing, however. If the bleeding does not stop within a few minutes with any wound, you should seek veterinary care.

c) Maintain Body Temperature.

Marsupials have a lower body temperature than humans. Keeping a constant body temperature is extremely important.

The average body temperature for most macropods is 95-97°F (35-36°C). Provide artificial heat only if the animal is hypothermic.

DO NOT allow a macropod to become overheated, the stress can be fatal. Overheated macropods should be allowed to cool down slowly.

(Please note that this precaution is absolutely critical in dealing with joeys, especially during the hand rearing phase of their lives. The babies have no way of regulating their own body temperature.)

d) Minimize Stress.

To minimize stress, keep your pet in a warm, quiet, and dark environment. Make sure there are no loud noises or sudden motions that will upset the animal even more.

If the animal is still young, place it in a pouch and then inside a box. For larger macropods, a blanket can be used to provide warmth and a sense of safety and security.

Concerns about stress with pet macropods don't just extend to situations of injury. In general, these animals do not like change. They become very accustomed to the constants in their environment and derive a sense of security from those things.

At any time that your pet wallaby or wallaroo seems to be exhibiting signs of illness or distress, evaluate its environment for stressors. Often simply eliminating something that is bothering the animal is the only "medicine" required.

Ch. 7) - Wallaby and Wallaroo Care Sheet

Keeping macropods like wallabies and wallaroos as pets can be a wonderful experience, but it can also be quite daunting, especially if you have never done it before.

While this book contains all of the information you need to care for your pets. The following is intended to serve as a quick reference resource.

1.) Basic Information

Scientific Classification: family Macropodidae, genus *Macropus*

Species: (See Chapter 1.)

Habitat: Australia, New Guinea, some nearby islands

Natural Environment: principally open country

Stature: upright with bent front legs

Temperament: curious and affectionate, can be mischievous

Diet: herbivorous, mainly grass and shrubs

Housing: large, fenced pen or pasture, must be well-secured

2.) Cage Set-up Guide

Enclosure Size: 820 feet^2 (250 m^2)

Additional Space: add 18 feet^2 (5.50 m^2) per animal

Fence Height: at least 6.5 feet (2 m) tall

Buried Fencing: 1.5 feet (0.5 m)

Additional Fencing Components: top 1.5 feet (0.5 m) hanging out at a 45-degree angle

Fencing Type: wire mesh or chain-link

Shelter Type: lean-to or shed/barn

Furnishings: logs, leafy branches, plastic cylinders, fast-growing shrubs

Substrate: grass, natural earth, rubber over concrete (temporary only)

Additional Requirements: holding areas for treatment/isolation

3.) Feeding Guide

Diet: herbivorous
Staples: grass, hay, shrubs
Supplements: commercial pellets, fresh vegetables

Water: always available, refreshed daily

Digestion Type: monogastic in youth, develops into fermentation-based

Adult Feed: equal parts alfalfa/Lucerne chaff, kangaroo muesli and kangaroo cubes

Food Presentation: clean containers

Food Containers: pellet bin/trough, chaff feeder/hay rack

4.) Breeding Information

Breeding Style: polygynous, opportunistic

Gestation Period: 30 to 38 days

Development in Pouch: 230 to 270 days

Nursing: 12 -14 months

Sexual Maturity (female): 14 to 24 months

Sexual Maturity (male): 18 to 20 months

Additional Facts: embryonic diapause allows female to become pregnant very shortly after birth

Ch. 8) - Additional Tips and Information

In this chapter you will find additional information regarding the care and keeping of Wallaroos. Some of the topics covered in this section are:

- Enclosure Maintenance Guidelines
- Conservation Status
- Determining Age in Macropods
- Rescuing Wild Joeys

1.) Enclosure Maintenance Guidelines

Hygiene is incredibly important when it comes to maintaining macropod enclosures. Not only do you need to wash your hands before handling or feeding your pets, but you also need to keep their habitat clean.

Feeding areas should be cleaned daily, and debris should be removed from the enclosure regularly. Refer to the following guidelines:

Daily Tasks:

- Refresh/refill water containers
- Clean out food troughs
- Rake feces from the yard
- Remove debris and branches that might cause injury
- Clear out leaf litter except in shady areas
- Remove dangerous/toxic weeds

Two to Three Times a Week

- Empty and scrub water containers
- Rinse and refill water containers
- Empty and disinfect food troughs
- Remove and replace bedding
- Clean food shed walls

To make your job easier, come up with a regular schedule for maintenance tasks. You may want to create a calendar and mark off the tasks you need to complete each day.

Keeping these records will help you to maintain a consistent schedule of upkeep. You can also use this calendar to keep track of treatments and reproductive stages.

Ch. 8) - Additional Tips and Information

2.) Conservation Status

Like many wild animals, wallabies and wallaroos have suffered from the expansion of human civilization, declining in numbers as a consequence of climate change and habitat destruction among other factors.

The following designations for conservation status were accurate at the time of this writing in late 2013, but may be subject to change at any time.

a) Wallabies

There are sixteen threatened species of rock wallabies in Australia. The Bridled Nail-Tail Wallaby is so endangered there are thought to be only 500 specimens left in the wild.

They are the victims of predation by other species including foxes and feral cats. One of the reasons Bennett's Wallabies are so popular as pets is their abundance and "least concern" status with the IUCN.

b) Common Wallaroo (*Macropus robustus*)

In 2008, the Common Wallaroo was assessed by the IUCN and given a status of "least concern." The animals are widely distributed and present in a number of protected areas.

The species lacks major threats and is unlikely to decline at a qualifying rate to be listed as "threatened."

c) Black Wallaroo (*Macropus bernardus*)

In 2008, the Black Wallaroo was assessed by the IUCN and given a status of "near threatened." This status was given because the global population is likely less than 10,000.

Though the population is probably stable, little is known about Black Wallaroo population trends. There are no known major threats to the species, though wildfires could be a problem in the future.

d) Antilopine Wallaroo (*Macropus antilopinus*)

In 2008, the Antilopine Wallaroo was assessed by the IUCN and given a status of "least concern." This status was given because the Antilopine Wallaroo is widely distributed and occurs in a number of protected areas.

The animals also lack any major threats and are unlikely to decline at a qualifying rate to be listed as "threatened."

3.) Determining Age in Macropods

The main method of age determination in adult macropods is molar eruption. The number of molars that remain in the jaw as well as the degree to which they are worn down, also help in establishing age. For younger animals, foot length and tail length are used to determine age.

On the next page I have created a chart which will provide an overview of the age progression in macropods.

Hopefully this chart will give you a better understanding of how to determine age.

Age Determination in Macropods		
Foot (mm)	**Tail (mm)**	**Age (in days)**
25	50	60
40	85	80
55	116	100
65	150	120
115	205	140
144	260	160
150	320	180
164	390	200
170	420	210

4.) Rescuing Wild Joeys

If you live in Australia, you may come across an abandoned joey while traveling country roads. Female macropods often have the misfortune to be hit by cars, dying on the side of the road with defenseless joeys in their pouch.

Stuck in their mother's pouch, not yet developed enough to survive on their own, the joey is likely to starve to death or become prey of predators. Though the joey can survive in the pouch for several days, their life expectancy is limited unless they are rescued.

If you come across an abandoned joey, your first step should be to assess it for injury. Wearing a pair of rubber gloves, check for cuts, abrasions and broken limbs. If the joey has broken limbs, it is unlikely to recover so it is kinder to euthanize the animal.

Although this preliminary examination is crucial, thereafter, handle the animal as little as possible. Although your intent will likely be to give comfort, the opposite will be true and you will only frighten the animal more.

Joeys are extremely susceptible to stress under the best of conditions, but if one is injured and already in shock, your attempts at comfort could be too much for the little animal to tolerate.

You should also check the joey's body temperature by feeling its feet – if the feet are cold, it is a sign that the body temperature is too low and the joey may be at risk for pneumonia.

Make sure to keep the joey warm as you transport it for veterinary care. Again, handle the animal as little as possible, placing it in some kind of temporary "pouch," like a warm, soft blanket for transport.

Ideally, you will place the joey in the pouch, and the pouch inside a cardboard box. This arrangement will enhance the animal's feeling of security and need for isolation.

From that point, follow the advice of the veterinary professionals regarding the animal's chances for survival. If you believe you can hand rear the animal, it is legal in Australia to do so.

Afterword

I certainly won't insult your intelligence by suggesting that you ever thought owning a wallaby or a wallaroo was, in any way, akin to bringing home a puppy or a kitten.

Now, at the end of this text, you hopefully understand even more fully the unique nature of marsupials and specifically of those marsupials that are members of the macropod family.

While wallabies and wallaroos are smaller than full-fledged kangaroos, all are active animals in need of adequate outdoor space. They are grazing herbivores that are, in many ways, rather like livestock.

That being said, however, a joey raised on a bottle can be one of the most affectionate and loyal creatures you'll ever encounter. Since it's highly recommended that foster joey parents literally wear the pouch in which their pet is snuggled, it's clear that in the joey's eyes, you become "Mum."

Some breeders have laughingly said that when they describe the hand-rearing process to friends the reaction is basically, "Why didn't you just have a baby?"

All pet owners are frank in their admission that much of the love they have for animals is invested in the unconditional affection they receive in return. Wallabies and wallaroos excel in that department, and consequently make superb companions.

They are not, however, house pets after the first year of life. They can come inside, and will enjoy doing so, but their primarily enclosure should be outside. Frankly, if you do not have land, you may want to reconsider your decision to be a macropod owner.

Part of the responsibility of keeping an exotic pet is meeting its needs in terms of diet, housing, and care. Not only can you not housebreak a wallaby or a wallaroo, you cannot expect it to confine its activities solely within the walls of a house, or, heaven forbid, an apartment.

If, however, your living circumstances are right, and there are no local legal impediments, you will find that life with a wallaby or wallaroo is both fun and rewarding. There is nothing "conventional" about either. They are intelligent, insatiably curious, often mischievous, and just plain fun.

Regardless of your decision for or against keeping wallabies and wallaroos, I hope you will come away from this reading with a new appreciation for these animals, and for their larger cousins the kangaroo.

Mankind once had the arrogant assumption that it was our role on this planet to exercise dominion over the animals. Now, thankfully, we have come to the realization that we live on a shared planet. We need animals and they need us.

Afterword

Sadly, many of our decisions have not been good ones for our animal friends. At least 16 species of rock wallabies are endangered, and many others are threatened. Habitat loss, climate change, and hunting have not served these creatures well.

Only by understanding the unique qualities of any species can we hope to protect and preserve it – and, in some cases, when the fit is right for all concerned, to make our lives in its company.

If there is a wallaby or a wallaroo in your future, you are about to see the world through different eyes. In the end, you'll be thankful for the view.

Relevant Websites

The following websites answer many additional questions about living with and caring for wallabies and wallaroos, as well as offering many delightful photos of the animals "in action."

At the time of this writing in late 2013, all of the sites were extant, but understand that the Internet is an ever-changing environment. Sites come and go, and I have no way of guaranteeing that this material will still be accessible in the future.

United States Websites:

"*Macropus Robustus* Hill Wallaroo." Animal Diversity Web – University of Michigan Museum of Zoology. www.animaldiversity.ummz.umich.edu/accounts/Macropus_robustus

"Common Wallaroo." World Association of Zoos and Aquariums. www.waza.org/en/zoo/pick-a-picture/macropus-robustus

"Euro or Common Wallaroo." Touring Australia. www.touringaustralia.de/Marsupials/Euro.php

Hyatt, Evan. "*Macropus Bernardus* Black Wallaroo." Animal Diversity Web – University of Michigan Museum of Zoology.

Relevant Websites

www.animaldiversity.ummz.umich.edu/accounts/Macropus_bernardus

"Wallaby – Animals Town"
www.animalstown.com/animals/w/wallaby/wallaby.html

"Treasure Ranch"
www.treasureranch.com/treasure/rzuinfofiles/wallabies.html

"Husbandry Guidelines for Agile Wallaby." Western Sydney Institute of TAFE, Richmond.
www.nswfmpa.org/Husbandry%20Manuals/Published%20Manuals/Mammalia/Agile%20Wallaby.pdf

"First Aid." Chidlow Marsupial Hospital, Inc.
www.chidlowmarsupialhospital.org.au/page-16.html

Ladds, Philip W. "Pathology of Macropods." Australian Registry of Wildlife Health.
www.arwh.org//sites/default/files/files-uploads/18%20Pathology%20of%20macropods.pdf

"Marsupials/Macropods." Wallaby Ranch.
www.wallabyranch.org/Marsupials-Macropods-PDF.pdf

"Wallaroo." Cleveland Metroparks Zoo.
www.clemetzoo.com/animals/index.asp?action=details&camefrom=alpha&animals_id=1223&strQuery=

"Macropus bernardus Black Wallaroo." Animal Diversity Web.
www.animaldiversity.ummz.umich.edu/accounts/Macropu s_bernardus

"Wallaroo." Rolling Hills Wildlife.
www.rollinghillswildlife.com/animals/w/wallaroo/wallaroo .pdf

"Wallaroos." Poway Unified School District.
www.powayusd.sdcoe.k12.ca.us/teachers/kjain/gallery/zoo s/zr/virtual%20zoo/wallaroo.html

"What Does a Wallaroo Eat?" PawNation.com.
www.animals.pawnation.com/walaroo-eat-2728.html

"Eastern Wallaroo." Oakland Zoo – Conservation and Education.
www.oaklandzoo.org/Eastern_Wallaroo.php

"Wallaroo." RollingHillsWildlife.com.
www.rollinghillswildlife.com/animals/w/wallaroo/wallaroo .pdf

"Husbandry Guidelines for Agile Wallaby." Western Sydney Institute of TAFE, Richmond.
www.nswfmpa.org/Husbandry%20Manuals/Published%20 Manuals/Mammalia/Agile%20Wallaby.pdf

"First Aid." Chidlow Marsupial Hospital, Inc.
www.chidlowmarsupialhospital.org.au/page-16.html

Ladds, Philip W. "Pathology of Macropods." Australian Registry of Wildlife Health. www.arwh.org//sites/default/files/files-uploads/18%20Pathology%20of%20macropods.pdf

"Marsupials/Macropods." Wallaby Ranch. wallabyranch.org/Marsupials-Macropods-PDF.pdf

"*Macropus Robustus* Hill Wallaroo." Animal Diversity Web – University of Michigan Museum of Zoology. www.animaldiversity.ummz.umich.edu/accounts/Macropus_robustus

"Common Wallaroo." World Association of Zoos and Aquariums. www.waza.org/en/zoo/pick-a-picture/macropus-robustus

"Euro or Common Wallaroo." Touring Australia. www.touringaustralia.de/Marsupials/Euro.php

Hyatt, Evan. "*Macropus Bernardus* Black Wallaroo." Animal Diversity Web – University of Michigan Museum of Zoology. www.animaldiversity.ummz.umich.edu/accounts/Macropus_bernardus

"Wallaroo." Cleveland Metroparks Zoo. www.clemetzoo.com/animals/index.asp?action=details&camefrom=alpha&animals_id=1223&strQuery=

"Macropus bernardus Black Wallaroo." Animal Diversity Web. www.animaldiversity.ummz.umich.edu/accounts/Macropus_bernardus

"Wallaroo." Rolling Hills Wildlife. www.rollinghillswildlife.com/animals/w/wallaroo/wallaroo.pdf

United Kingdom Websites:

"How to Own a Pet Wallaroo." eHow.co.uk. www.ehow.co.uk/how_2056664_own-pet-wallaroo.html

"Kangaroos, Wallabies and Wallaroos." BBC Nature – Wildlife. www.bbc.co.uk/nature/life/Macropus

"Introduction to the Care and Handraising of Macropods." The Northern Tablelands Wildlife Carers, Inc. www.training.ntwc.org.au/PDF/Macropod_Care.pdf

"Housing." Chidlow Marsupial Hospital. www.chidlowmarsupialhospital.org.au/page-21-1-housing.html

"Common Injuries and Diseases." Chidlow Marsupial Hospital. www.chidlowmarsupialhospital.org.au/page-44-1-common-injuries.html

"First Aid." Chidlow Marsupial Hospital, Inc.
www.chidlowmarsupialhospital.org.au/page-16.html

"Herpesviruses and Macropods Fact Sheet." Australian
Wildlife Health Network.
www.wildlifehealth.org.au/Portals/0/Documents/FactSheet
s/Herpesviruses%20(Macropods)%201%20Apr%202012%20
(1.0).pdf

"Handbook for Kangaroo Harvesters." The Department of
Environment, Climate Change and Water.
www.environment.nsw.gov.au/resources/nature/kmp/1016
0Hbkangharvesters.pdf

"Common Wallaroo." Online Encyclopedia.
www.encyclo.co.uk/define/Common%20wallaroo

"Australian Mammals, July 2000."
WildelifeontheWeb.co.uk.
www.wildlifeontheweb.co.uk/pdf/AustraliaMammals2000.
pdf

Latham, Enid. "Introduction to the Care and Handraising
of Macropods." www.training.ntwc.org.au/PDF/
Macropod_Care.pdf

"Antilopine Wallaroo." Australian Wildlife Conservancy.
www.australianwildlife.org/Wildlife-and-
Ecosystems/Wildlife-Profiles/Mammals/Antilopine-
Wallaroo.aspx

"Diet of Four Rock-Dwelling Macropods in the Australian Monsoon Tropics." British Library Document Supply Service. www.bldss.bl.uk/BLDSS/?searchRecordID=ETOCRN195416 411#/New%20Order/0

"How to Own a Pet Wallaroo." eHow.co.uk. www.ehow.co.uk/how_2056664_own-pet-wallaroo.html

"Kangaroos, Wallabies and Wallaroos." BBC Nature – Wildlife. www.bbc.co.uk/nature/life/Macropus

"Introduction to the Care and Handraising of Macropods." The Northern Tablelands Wildlife Carers, Inc. www.training.ntwc.org.au/PDF/Macropod_Care.pdf

"Housing." Chidlow Marsupial Hospital. www.chidlowmarsupialhospital.org.au/page-21-1-housing.html

"Common Injuries and Diseases." Chidlow Marsupial Hospital. www.chidlowmarsupialhospital.org.au/page-44-1-common-injuries.html

"First Aid." Chidlow Marsupial Hospital, Inc. www.chidlowmarsupialhospital.org.au/page-16.html

"Herpesviruses and Macropods Fact Sheet." Australian Wildlife Health Network. www.wildlifehealth.org.au/Portals/0/Documents/FactSheet

s/Herpesviruses%20(Macropods)%201%20Apr%202012%20
(1.0).pdf>

"Handbook for Kangaroo Harvesters." The Department of
Environment, Climate Change and Water.
www.environment.nsw.gov.au/resources/nature/kmp/1016
0Hbkangharvesters.pdf

"Common Wallaroo." Online Encyclopedia.
www.encyclo.co.uk/define/Common%20wallaroo

"Australian Mammals, July 2000."
WildelifeontheWeb.co.uk.
www.wildlifeontheweb.co.uk/pdf/AustraliaMammals2000.
pdf

Latham, Enid. "Introduction to the Care and Handraising
of Macropods." www.training.ntwc.org.au/PDF/
Macropod_Care.pdf

"Antilopine Wallaroo." Australian Wildlife Conservancy.
www.australianwildlife.org/Wildlife-and-
Ecosystems/Wildlife-Profiles/Mammals/Antilopine-
Wallaroo.aspx

Frequently Asked Questions

Although I recommend you read the entire text to understand the truly unique nature of wallabies and wallaroos, the following are some of the most frequently asked questions about these charming macropods.

Do wallabies and wallaroos make good pets?

Yes, they do. In fact, you will be surprised by just how affectionate and loyal a hand-reared joey will become as it matures. Understand, however, that if you are raising the animal from a young age, you are taking on a commitment not unlike that of a newborn baby.

A joey depends strongly on a sense of security with his "mother," which will be you. One of the best ways to bond with a joey, and to ensure its well-being at all times is simply to put the baby in his pouch and wear the pouch.

While that may not be possible at every hour of your day, the more you can care from the joey in this way, the more likely the chances that the little one will thrive.

During the first year of life, you can typically keep your pet inside, but as it grows, an outside enclosure will become a necessity.

How do wallabies and wallaroos get along with other pets and children?

The more accurate question might be to ask how the other animals and the children will get along with the macropod. It's very difficult to predict how domestic animals will react to a wallaby or wallaroo, so the animals should never be left unsupervised.

A joey can be seriously injured by a family dog that is not being aggressive, but is simply playing too hard.

It is imperative that joeys NOT be kept with cats, since feline feces can contain the protozoan that causes toxoplasmosis, a condition that is fatal to joeys.

As is the case with all pets, young children should be taught to interact with the joey with kindness and respect. A joey has delicate bones and is subject to stress, especially at a young age, facts of which children should be made aware. Again, supervision is recommended.

How much and how often should I feed my joey?

Macropod mothers have the ability to vary the composition of their milk according to the nutritional needs of the joey at each stage of its development.

The manufacturers of supplemental feeds attempt to duplicate this process, and thus sell their products according to systems of growth charts that guide surrogate macropod parents in the selection of feed as well as in how much should be dispensed according to age.

It is recommended that you follow the directions on the supplemental product you are using to the letter. If you acquired your joey from a breeder, rely on that person for advice both on products and procedures in feeding a young macropod.

How do I "toilet" my joey?

In the wild a joey's mother will stimulate urination and defecation in her young by licking the baby's genital region. You can replicate this process by gently tapping or lightly stroking the area with a tissue or warm washcloth.

After the joey has fed or awakens from a nap, carry the animal to the toilet and hold it gently but securely over the bowl. Stimulate the joey until it is completely finished urinating or defecating. This may take a few minutes since the animals urinate with a spurting action rather than a steady stream.

It is extremely important to toilet the joey regularly as failure to do so can lead to urinary tract, kidney, and bowel disease.

Can wallabies and wallaroos be housebroken?

While some owners claim that they have successfully housebroken their joeys, most breeders say that this is not possible. Generally when a joey becomes too large to toilet successfully, it's time to consider an outdoor enclosure.

Why are playpens recommended for joeys?

A child's mesh playpen is essential in raising joeys not only for your convenience in containing the animal when you can't supervise it, but also for the joey's comfort and safety.

The joey's pouch can be secured to the side of the playpen so the little animal can hop in and out at will, but be in a private and limited area.

(Note that when hanging a joey's pouch that the bottom should not touch the floor.)

When should a joey be weaned?

Many breeders believe that a joey should be allowed to take a bottle as long as they are interested doing so. In time, the animal will begin to show an interest in solid food on its own.

When a joey becomes interested in solid food, what should I give it to help it get off the bottle?

When a joey starts to lose interest in the bottle, offer your pet some green grass to get him used to chewing. Once he's doing that reliably, you can move to the hay and pellet foods that will be his nutritional staples for life. (See Chapter 4 for more information on feeding and nutrition.)

Glossary

B

buck – Common term for a male macropod. Also called a boomer or a jack.

boomer - Common term for a male macropod, also called a buck or a jack.

C

conception – the meeting of sperm and ovum to create a fetus (baby)

D

diapause - A behavior in some insects, invertebrates, and mammals that allows for the suspension of the development of an embryo due to unfavorable environmental conditions or, in the case of macropods, the presence of another offspring in a later stage of development in the marsupium.

doe – A common term for a female macropod, also called a jill.

E

estrus cycle – The regularly occurring period of fertility when a female of any species is producing eggs and is receptive to mating with a male.

G

gestation – That period of time during which a fetus of any species develops inside the female's womb inside a protective placenta. This does not occur in macropods. The baby, termed a neonate, emerges from the womb at birth and climbs into the pouch where it finishes its development.

H

herbivores - Animals that consume plants as a primary means of subsistence.

hybridization – The cross-breeding of two different species or subspecies to produce a unique hybrid offspring.

J

jack – Common term for a male macropod, also called a buck or a boomer.

jill - Common term for a female macropod, also called a doe.

joey – Common term for a baby macropod.

K

kangaroo - The largest members of the family of marsupials called "macropods" short for *Macropodidae*.

M

macropod – An animal belonging to the family of marsupials. Macropods include kangaroos, wallaroos, wallabies, tree-kangaroos and pademelons. The term "macropod" translates literally as "large foot."

marsupial – A type of mammal that carries its young in a pouch or marsupium as it develops

marsupium - The pouch of a female marsupial where the baby or joey finishes its development after emerging from the womb as a partially developed neonate.

N

neonate - The partially developed young of a marsupial that emerges from the womb at birth to crawl into the mother's pouch or marsupium to complete its development.

P

pademelon - A species of forest-dwelling wallaby.

polygynous – A mating system in which males have more than one female partner.

portmanteau - A word form in which two sounds and meanings of different words are combined to create a new meaning as in "wallaby" and "kangaroo" to arrive at "wallaroo."

R

ruminant - Mammals that regurgitate their food as rumen, which they chew as "cud."

S

subspecies – Variations of the same species, generally classified by geographical location.

W

wallaby - A name used informally for about 30 macropods that are physically smaller than both kangaroos and wallaroos.

wallaroo - A combination of the words "wallaby" and "kangaroo" to describe animals of an intermediate size in the macropod family. Note that this term is not used in Australia.

Index

Lightning Source UK Ltd.
Milton Keynes UK
UKHW020740130319
339054UK00014B/776/P